THE POPOL VUH

DOVER THRIFT EDITIONS

Translated and Edited by
Lewis Spence

DOVER PUBLICATIONS, INC.
MINEOLA, NEW YORK

DOVER THRIFT EDITIONS

GENERAL EDITOR: SUSAN L. RATTINER
EDITOR OF THIS VOLUME: JANET B. KOPITO

Bibliographical Note

This Dover edition, first published in 2019, is an unabridged
republication of the work published by David Nutt, London, in 1908.

International Standard Book Number

ISBN-13: 978-0-486-83664-5
ISBN-10: 0-486-83664-9

Manufactured in the United States by LSC Communications
83664901
www.doverpublications.com

2 4 6 8 10 9 7 5 3 1

2019

Contents

PREFACE

THE "POPOL VUH" is the New World's richest mythological mine. No translation of it has as yet appeared in English, and no adequate translation in any European language. It has been neglected to a certain extent because of the unthinking strictures passed upon its authenticity. That other manuscripts exist in Guatemala than the one discovered by Ximenes and transcribed by Scherzer and Brasseur de Bourbourg is probable. So thought Brinton, and the present writer shares his belief. And ere it is too late it would be well that these—the only records of the faith of the builders of the mystic ruined and deserted cities of Central America—should be recovered. This is not a matter that should be left to the enterprise of individuals, but one which should engage the consideration of interested governments; for what is myth to-day is often history to-morrow.

PREFACE

THE POPOL VUH

[The numbers in the text refer to notes at the end of the study]

THERE IS NO document of greater importance to the study of the pre-Columbian mythology of America than the "Popol Vuh." It is the chief source of our knowledge of the mythology of the Kiché people of Central America, and it is further of considerable comparative value when studied in conjunction with the mythology of the Nahuatlacâ, or Mexican peoples. This interesting text, the recovery of which forms one of the most romantic episodes in the history of American bibliography, was written by a Christianised native of Guatemala some time in the seventeenth century, and was copied in the Kiché language, in which it was originally written, by a monk of the Order of Predicadores, one Francisco Ximenes, who also added a Spanish translation and scholia.

The Abbé Brasseur de Bourbourg, a profound student of American archæology and languages (whose euhemeristic interpretations of the Mexican myths are as worthless as the priceless materials he unearthed are valuable) deplored, in a letter to the Duc de Valmy,[1] the supposed loss of the "Popol Vuh," which he was aware had been made use of early in the nineteenth

---

[1]   Mexico, Oct. 15, 1850.

1

century by a certain Don Felix Cabrera. Dr. C. Scherzer, an Austrian scholar, thus made aware of its value, paid a visit to the Republic of Guatemala in 1854 or 1855, and was successful in tracing the missing manuscript in the library of the University of San Carlos in the city of Guatemala. It was afterwards ascertained that its scholiast, Ximenes, had deposited it in the library of his convent at Chichicastenango whence it passed to the San Carlos library in 1830.

Scherzer at once made a copy of the Spanish translation of the manuscript, which he published at Vienna in 1856 under the title of "Las Historias del origen de los Indios de Guatemala, par el R. P. F. Francisco Ximenes." The Abbé Brasseur also took a copy of the original, which he published at Paris in 1861, with the title "Vuh Popol: Le Livre Sacré de Quichés, et les Mythes de l'Antiquité Américaine." In this work the Kiché original and the Abbé's French translation are set forth side by side. Unfortunately both the Spanish and the French translations leave much to be desired so far as their accuracy is concerned,* and they are rendered of little use by reason of the misleading notes which accompany them.

The name "Popol Vuh" signifies "Record of the Community," and its literal translation is "Book of the Mat," from the Kiché words "pop" or "popol," a mat or rug of woven rushes or bark on which the entire family sat, and "vuh" or "uuh," paper or book, from "uoch" to write. The "Popol Vuh" is an example of a world-wide genre—a type of annals of which the first portion is pure mythology, which gradually shades off into pure history, evolving from the hero-myths of saga to the recital of the deeds of authentic personages. It may, in fact, be classed with the Heimskringla

---

*   See p. 51, Section I, lines 5–8.

of Snorre, the Danish History of Saxo-Grammaticus, the Chinese History in the Five Books, the Japanese "Nihongi," and, so far as its fourth book is concerned, it somewhat resembles the Pictish Chronicle.

The language in which the "Popol Vuh" was written was, as has been said, the Kiché, a dialect of the great Maya-Kiché tongue spoken at the time of the Conquest from the borders of Mexico on the north to those of the present State of Nicaragua on the south; but whereas the Mayan was spoken in Yucatan proper, and the State of Chiapas, the Kiché was the tongue of the peoples of that part of Central America now occupied by the States of Guatemala, Honduras and San Salvador, where it is still used by the natives. It is totally different to the Nahuatl, the language of the peoples of Anahuac or Mexico, both as regards its origin and structure, and its affinities with other American tongues are even less distinct than those between the Slavonic and Teutonic groups. Of this tongue the "Popol Vuh" is practically the only monument; at all events the only work by a native of the district in which it was used. A cognate dialect, the Cakchiquel, produced the "Annals" of that people, otherwise known as "The Book of Chilan Balam," a work purely of genealogical interest, which may be consulted in the admirable translation of the late Daniel G. Brinton.

The Kiché people at the time of their discovery, which was immediately subsequent to the fall of Mexico, had in part lost that culture which was characteristic of the Mayan race, the remnants of which have excited universal wonder in the ruins of the vast desert cities of Central America (Note 1). At a period not far distant from the Conquest the once centralised Government of the Mayan peoples had been broken up into petty States and Confederacies, which in their character recall the city-states of mediæval Italy. In all probability the civilisation possessed by these peoples had been brought them by a race from Mexico called the Toltecs (Note 2), who taught them the arts of building in stone and writing in hieroglyphics, and who probably influenced their mythology most profoundly. The Toltecs were not, however, in any way cognate with the Mayans, and were in all likelihood rapidly absorbed by them. The Mayans were notably an agricultural people, and it is not impossible that in their country the maize-plant was first cultivated with the object of obtaining a regular cereal supply (Note 3).

Such, then, were the people whose mythology produced the body of tradition and mythi-history known as the "Popol Vuh"; and ere we pass to a consideration of their beliefs, their gods, and their religious affinities, it will be well to summarise the three books of it which treat of these things, as fully as space will permit, using for that purpose both the French translation of Brasseur and the Spanish one of Ximenes.

THE FIRST BOOK

OVER A UNIVERSE wrapped in the gloom of a dense and primeval night passed the god Hurakan, the mighty wind. He called out "earth," and the solid land appeared. The chief gods took counsel; they were Hurakan, Gucumatz, the serpent covered with green feathers, and Xpiyacoc and Xmucane, the mother and father gods. As the result of their deliberations animals were created. But as yet man was not. To supply the deficiency the divine beings resolved to create mannikins carved out of wood. But these soon incurred the displeasure of the gods, who, irritated by their lack of reverence, resolved to destroy them. Then by the will of Hurakan, the Heart of Heaven, the waters were swollen, and a great flood came upon the mannikins of wood. They were drowned and a thick resin fell from heaven. The bird Xecotcovach tore out their eyes; the bird Camulatz cut off their heads; the bird Cotzbalam devoured their flesh; the bird Tecumbalam broke their bones and sinews and ground them into powder. Because they had not thought on Hurakan, therefore the face of the earth grew dark, and a pouring rain commenced, raining by day and by night. Then all sorts of beings, great and small, gathered together to abuse the men to their faces. The very household utensils and animals jeered at them, their mill-stones, their plates, their cups, their dogs, their hens. Said the dogs and hens, "Very badly have you treated us, and you have bitten us.

5

Now we bite you in turn." Said the mill-stones (metates[1]), "Very much were we tormented by you, and daily, daily, night and day, it was *squeak, screech, screech,*[2] for your sake. Now you shall feel our strength, and we will grind your flesh and make meal of your bodies." And the dogs upbraided the mannikins because they had not been fed, and tore the unhappy images with their teeth. And the cups and dishes said, "Pain and misery you gave us, smoking our tops and sides, cooking us over the fire burning and hurting us as if we had no feeling. Now it is your turn, and you shall burn." Then ran the mannikins hither and thither in despair. They climbed to the roofs of the houses, but the houses crumbled under their feet; they tried to mount to the tops of the trees, but the trees hurled them from them; they sought refuge in the caverns, but the caverns closed before them. Thus was accomplished the ruin of this race, destined to be overthrown. And it is said that their posterity are the little monkeys who live in the woods.

THE MYTH OF VUKUB-CAKIX

After this catastrophe, ere yet the earth was quite recovered from the wrath of the gods, there existed a man "full of pride," whose name was Vukub-Cakix. The name signifies "Seven-times-the-colour-of-fire," or "Very brilliant," and was justified by the fact that its owner's eyes were of silver, his teeth of emerald, and other parts of his anatomy of precious metals. In his own opinion Vukub-Cakix's existence rendered unnecessary that of the sun and the moon, and this egoism so disgusted the gods that they

---

[1]   Large hollowed stones used by the women for bruising maize.

[2]   The Kiché words are onomatopoetic—"holi, holi, huqi, huqi."

resolved upon his overthrow. His two sons, Zipacna and Cabrakan (earth-heaper[1] (?) and earthquake), were daily employed, the one in heaping up mountains, and the other in demolishing thorn, and these also incurred the wrath of the immortals. Shortly after the decision of the deities the twin hero-gods Hun-Ahpu and Xbalanque came to earth with the intention of chastising the arrogance of Vukub-Cakix and his progeny.

Now Vukub-Cakix had a great tree of the variety known in Central America as "nanze" or "tapal," bearing a fruit round, yellow, and aromatic, and upon this fruit he depended for his daily sustenance. One day on going to partake of it for his morning meal he mounted to its summit in order to espy the choicest fruits, when to his great indignation he discovered that Hun-Ahpu and Xbalanque had been before him, and had almost denuded the tree of its produce. The hero-gods, who lay concealed within the foliage, now added injury to theft by hurling at Vukub-Cakix a dart from a blow-pipe, which had the effect of precipitating him from the summit of the tree to the earth. He arose in great wrath, bleeding profusely from a severe wound in the jaw. Hun-Ahpu then threw himself upon Vukub-Cakix, who in terrible anger seized the god by the arm and wrenched it from the body. He then proceeded to his dwelling, where he was met and anxiously interrogated by his spouse Chimalmat. Tortured by the pain in his teeth and jaw he, in an access of spite, hung Hun-Ahpu's arm over a blazing fire, and then threw himself down to bemoan his injuries, consoling himself, however, with the idea that he had adequately avenged himself upon the interlopers who had dared to disturb his peace.

---

[1] Zipac signifies "Cockspur," and I take the name to signify also "Thrower-up of earth." The connection is obvious.

But Hun-Ahpu and Xbalanque were in no mind that he should escape so easily, and the recovery of Hun-Ahpu's arm must be made at all hazards. With this end in view they consulted two venerable beings in whom we readily recognise the father-mother divinities, Xpiyacoc and Xmucane (Note 4), disguised for the nonce as sorcerers. These personages accompanied Hun-Ahpu and Xbalanque to the abode of Vukub-Cakix, whom they found in a state of intense agony. The ancients persuaded him to be operated upon in order to relieve his sufferings, and for his glittering teeth they substituted grains of maize. Next they removed his eyes of emerald, upon which his death speedily followed, as did that of his wife Chimalmat. Hun-Ahpu's arm was recovered, re-affixed to his shoulder, and all ended satisfactorily for the hero-gods.

But their mission was not yet complete. The sons of Vukub-Cakix, Zipacna and Cabrakan, remained to be accounted for. Zipacna consented, at the entreaty of four hundred youths, incited by the hero-gods, to assist them in transporting a huge tree which was destined for the roof-tree of a house they were building. Whilst assisting them he was beguiled by them into entering a great ditch which they had dug for the purpose of destroying him, and when once he descended was overwhelmed by tree-trunks by his treacherous acquaintances, who imagined him to be slain. But he took refuge in a side-tunnel of the excavation, cut off his hair and nails for the ants to carry up to his enemies as a sign of his death, waited until the youths had become intoxicated with pulque because of joy at his supposed demise, and then, emerging from the pit, shook the house that the youths had built over his body about their heads, so that all were destroyed in its ruins.

But Run-Ahpu and Xbalanque were grieved that the four hundred had perished, and laid a more efficacious trap for

Zipacna. The mountain-bearer, carrying the mountains by night, sought his sustenance by day by the shore of the river, where he lived upon fish and crabs. The hero-gods constructed an artificial crab which they placed in a cavern at the bottom of a deep ravine. The hungry titan descended to the cave, which he entered on all-fours. But a neighbouring mountain had been undermined by the divine brothers, and its bulk was cast upon him. Thus at the foot of Mount Meavan perished the proud "Mountain Maker," whose corpse was turned into stone by the catastrophe.

Of the family of boasters only Cabrakan remained. Discovered by the hero-gods at his favourite pastime of overturning the hills, they enticed him in an easterly direction, challenging him to overthrow a particularly high mountain. On the way they shot a bird with their blow-pipes, and poisoned it with earth. This they gave to Cabrakan to eat. After partaking of the poisoned fare his strength deserted him, and failing to move the mountain he was bound and buried by the victorious hero-gods.

THE SECOND BOOK

MYSTERY VEILS THE commencement of the Second Book of the "Popol Vuh." The theme is the birth and family of Hun-Ahpu and Xbalanque, and the scribe intimates that only half is to be told concerning the history of their father. Xpiyacoc and Xmucane, the father and mother deities, had two sons, Hunhun-Ahpu and Vukub-Hunahpu, the first being, so far as can be gathered, a bi-sexual personage. He had by a wife, Xbakiyalo, two sons, Hunbatz and Hunchouen, men full of wisdom and artistic genius. All of them were addicted to the recreation of dicing and playing at ball, and a spectator of their pastimes was Voc, the messenger of Hurakan. Xbakiyalo having died, Hunhun-Ahpu and Vukub-Hunahpu, leaving the former's sons behind, played a game of ball which in its progress took them into the vicinity of the realm of Xibalba (the underworld). This reached the ears of the monarchs of that place, Hun-Came and Vukub-Came, who, after consulting their counsellors, challenged the strangers to a game of ball, with the object of defeating and disgracing them.

For this purpose they dispatched four messengers in the shape of owls. The brothers accepted the challenge, after a touching farewell with their mother Xmucane, and their sons and nephews, and followed the feathered heralds down the steep incline to Xibalba from the playground at Ninxor

Carchah.[1] After an ominous crossing over a river of blood they came to the residence of the kings of Xibalba, where they underwent the mortification of mistaking two wooden figures for the monarchs. Invited to sit on the seat of honour, they discovered it to be a red-hot stone, and the contortions which resulted from their successful trick caused unbounded merriment among the Xibalbans. Then they were thrust into the House of Gloom, where they were sacrificed and buried. The head of Hunhun-Ahpu was, however, suspended from a tree, which speedily became covered with gourds, from which it was almost impossible to distinguish the bloody trophy. All in Xibalba were forbidden the fruit of that tree.

But one person in Xibalba had resolved to disobey the mandate. This was the virgin princess Xquiq (Blood), the daughter of Cuchumaquiq, who went unattended to the spot. Standing under the branches gazing at the fruit, the maiden stretched out her hand, and the head of Hunhun-Ahpu spat into the palm. The spittle caused her to conceive, and she returned home, being assured by the head of the hero-god that no harm should result to her. This thing was done by order of Hurakan, the Heart of Heaven. In six months' time her father became aware of her condition, and despite her protestations the royal messengers of Xibalba, the owls, received orders to kill her and return with her heart in a vase. She, however, escaped by bribing the owls with splendid promises for the future to spare her and substitute for her heart the coagulated sap of the blood-wart.

In her extremity Xquiq went for protection to the home of Xmucane, who now looked after the Young Hunbatz and Hunchouen. Xmucane would not at first believe her tale. But

---

[1] Near Vera Paz.

Xquiq appealed to the gods, and performed a miracle by gathering a basket of maize where no maize grew, and thus gained her confidence.

Shortly afterwards Xquiq became the mother of twin boys, the heroes of the First Book, Hun-Ahpu, and Xbalanque. These did not find favour in the eyes of Xmucane, their grandmother. Their infantile cries aroused the wrath of this venerable person, and she vented it upon them by turning them out of doors. They speedily took to an outdoor life, however, and became mighty hunters, and expert in the use of their blowpipes, with which they shot birds and other small game. The ill-treatment which they received from Hunbatz; and Hunchouen caused them at last to retaliate, and those who had made their lives miserable were punished by being transformed by the divine children into apes. The venerable Xmucane, filled with grief at the metamorphosis and flight of her ill-starred grandsons, who had made her home joyous with their singing and flute-playing, was told that she would be permitted to behold their faces once more if she could do so without losing her gravity, but their antics and grimaces caused her such merriment that on three separate occasions she was unable to restrain her laughter and the Men-Monkeys appeared no more. Hun-Ahpu and Xbalanque now became expert musicians, and one of their favourite airs was that of "Hun-Ahpu qoy," the "monkey of Hun-Ahpu."

The divine twins were now old enough to undertake labour in the field, and their first task was the clearing of a milpa or maize-plantation. They were possessed of magic tools, which had the merit of working themselves in the absence of the young hunters at the chase, and those they found a capital substitute for their own directing presence upon the first day. Returning at night from hunting, they smeared their faces and hands with dirt so that Xmucane might be deceived into imagining that they had been hard at work in the maize-field. But during the night the wild beasts met and replaced all the roots and shrubs which the brothers—or rather their magic tools—had removed. The twins resolved to watch for them on the ensuing night, but despite all their efforts the animals succeeded in making good their escape, save one, the rat, which was caught in a handkerchief. The rabbit and deer lost their tails in getting away. The rat, in gratitude that they had spared its life, told them of the glorious deeds of their great fathers and uncles, their games at ball, and of the existence of a set of implements necessary to play the game which they had left in the house. They discovered these, and went to play in the ball-ground of their fathers.

It was not long, however, until Hun-Came and Vukub-Came, the princes of Xibalba, heard them at play, and decided to lure them to the Underworld as they had lured their fathers. Messengers were despatched to the house of Xmucane, who, filled with alarm, despatched a louse to carry the message to her grandsons. The louse, wishing to ensure greater speed to reach the brothers, consented to be swallowed by a toad, the toad by a serpent, and the serpent by the great bird Voc. The other animals duly liberated one another; but despite his utmost efforts, the toad could not get rid of the louse, who had played him a trick by lodging in his gums, and had not been swallowed at all. The message, however, was duly delivered, and the players returned home to take leave of their grandmother and mother. Before their departure they each planted a cane in the middle of the house, which was to acquaint those they left behind with their welfare, since it would wither if any fatal circumstance befell them.

Pursuing the route their fathers had followed, they passed the river of blood and the river Papuhya. But they sent an animal called Xan as *avant courier* with orders to prick all the Xibalbans with a hair from Hun-Ahpu's leg, thus discovering those of the dwellers in the Underworld who were made of wood—those whom their fathers had unwittingly bowed to as men—and also learning the names of the others by their inquiries and explanations when pricked. Thus they did not salute the mannikins on their arrival at the Xibalban court, nor did they sit upon the red-hot stone. They even passed scatheless through the first ordeal of the House of Gloom. The Xibalbans were furious, and their wrath was by no means allayed when they found themselves beaten at the game of ball to which they had challenged the brothers. Then Hun-Came and Vukub-Came ordered the twins to bring them four bouquets of flowers, asking the guards of the royal gardens to watch most carefully, and committed Hun-Ahpu and Xbalanque to the "House of Lances"—the second ordeal—where the lancers were directed to kill them. The brothers, however, had at their beck and call a swarm of ants, which entered the royal gardens on the first errand, and they succeeded in bribing the lancers. The Xibalbans, white with fury, ordered that the owls, the guardians of the gardens, should have their lips split, and otherwise showed their anger at their third defeat.

Then came the third ordeal in the "House of Cold." Here the heroes escaped death by freezing by being warmed with burning pine-cones. In the fourth and fifth ordeals they were equally lucky, for they passed a night each in the "House of Tigers" and the "House of Fire" without injury. But at the sixth ordeal misfortune overtook them in the "House of Bats." Hun-Ahpu's head being cut off by Camazotz, "Rule of Bats," who suddenly appeared from above.

The beheading of Hun-Ahpu does not, however, appear to have terminated fatally, but owing to the unintelligible nature of the text at this juncture, it is impossible to ascertain in what manner he was cured of such a lethal wound. This episode is followed by an assemblage of all the animals, and another contest at ball-playing, after which the brothers emerged uninjured from all the ordeals of the Xibalbans.

But in order to further astound their "hosts," Hun-Ahpu and Xbalanque confided to two sorcerers named Xulu and Pacaw that the Xibalbans had failed because the animals were not on their side, and directing them what to do with their bones, they stretched themselves upon a funeral pile and died together. Their bones were beaten to powder and thrown into the river, where they sank, and were transformed into young men. On the fifth day they reappeared like men-fishes, and on the sixth in the form of ragged old men, dancing, burning and restoring houses, killing and restoring each other to life, with other wonders. The princes of Xibalba, bearing of their skill, requested them to exhibit their magical powers, which they did by burning the royal palace and restoring it, killing and resuscitating the king's dog, and cutting a man in pieces, and bringing him to life again. The monarchs of Xibalba, anxious to experience the novel sensation of a temporary death, requested to be slain and resuscitated. They were speedily killed, but the brothers refrained from resuscitating their archenemies.

Announcing their real names, the brothers proceeded to punish the princes of Xibalba. The game of ball was forbidden them, they were to perform menial tasks, and only the beasts of the forest were they to hold in vassalage. They appear after this to achieve a species of doubtful distinction as plutonic deities or demons. They are described as warlike, ugly as owls,

inspiring evil and discord. Their faces were painted black and white to show their faithless nature.

Xmucane, waiting at home for the brothers, was alternately filled with joy and grief as the canes grow green and withered, according to the varying fortunes of her grandsons. These young men were busied at Xibalba with paying fitting funeral honours to their father and uncle, who now mounted to heaven and became the sun and moon, whilst the four hundred youths slain by Zipacna became the stars. Thus concludes the second book.

THE THIRD BOOK

THE BEGINNING OF the third book finds the gods once more in council. In the darkness they commune concerning the creation of man. The Creator and Former made four perfect men. These beings were wholly created from yellow and White maize. Their names were Balam-Quitzé (Tiger with the Sweet Smile), Balam-Agab (Tiger of the Night), Mahucutah (The Distinguished Name), and Iqi-Balam. (Tiger of the Moon). They had neither father nor mother, neither were they made by the ordinary agents in the work of creation. Their creation was a miracle of the Former.[1]

But Hurakan was not altogether satisfied with his handiwork. These men were too perfect. They knew overmuch. Therefore the gods took counsel as to how to proceed with man. They must not become as gods (note here the Christian influence). Let us now contract their sight so that they may only be able to see a portion of the earth and be content, said the gods. Then Hurakan breathed a cloud over their eyes, which became partially veiled. Then the four men slept, and four women were made, Caha-Paluma (Falling Water), Choimha (Beautiful Water), Tzununiha (House of the Water), and Cakixa (Water of Aras or Parrots), who became the wives of the men in their respective order as mentioned above.

---

[1] Hurakan.

19

These were the ancestors of the Kichés only. Then were created the ancestors of other peoples. They were ignorant of the methods of worship, and lifting their eyes to heaven prayed to the Creator, the Former, for peaceable lives and the return of the sun. But no sun came, and they grew uneasy. So they set out for Tulan-Zuiva, or the Seven Caves, and there gods were given unto them, each man, as head of a group of the race, a god. Balam-Quitzé received the god Tohil. Balam-Agab received the god Avilix, and Mahucutah the god Hacavitz. Iqi-Balam received a god, but as he had no family his god is not taken into account in the native mythology.

The Kichés now began to feel the want of fire, and the god Tohil, the creator of fire, supplied them with this element. But soon afterwards a mighty rain extinguished all the fires in the land. Tohil, however, always renewed the supply. And fire in those days was the chief necessity, for as yet there was no sun.

Tulan was a place of misfortune to man, for not only did he suffer from cold and famine, but here his speech was so confounded that the first four men were no longer able to comprehend each other. They determined to leave Tulan, and under the leadership of the god Tohil set out to search for a new abode. On they wandered through innumerable hardships. Many mountains had they to climb, and a long passage to make through the sea which was miraculously divided for their journey from shore to shore. At length they came to a mountain which they called Hacavitz, after one of their gods, and here they rested, for here they had been instructed that they should see the sun. And the sun appeared. Animals and men were transported with delight. All the celestial bodies were now established. But the sun was not as it is to-day. He was not strong, but as reflected in a mirror.

As he arose the three tribal gods were turned into stone, as were the gods—probably totems—connected with the wild animals. Then arose the first Kiché city.

As time progressed the first men grew old, and, impelled by visions, they began to offer human sacrifices. For this purpose they raided the villages of the neighbouring peoples, who retaliated. But by the miraculous aid of a horde of wasps and hornets the Kichés utterly routed their enemies. And the aliens became tributory to them.

Now it came nigh the death-time of the first men, and they called their descendants together to hearken unto their last counsels. In the anguish of their hearts they sang the Kamucu, the song "We see," that they had sung when it first became light. Then they took leave of their wives and sons, one by one. And suddenly they were not. But in their place was a huge bundle, which was never unfolded. And it was called the "Majesty Enveloped." And so died the first men of the Kichés.

THE FOURTH BOOK

THE FOURTH BOOK brings us down to what is presumably history. We say "presumably," because we have only the bare testimony of the "Popol Vuh" to go upon. We can note therein the evolution of the Kiché people from a comparatively simple and pastoral state of society to a political condition of considerable complexity. This account of the later periods is extremely confused, and as the names of many of the Kiché monarchs are the same as those of the gods, it is often difficult to discriminate between saga and history. Interminable conflicts are the subject of most of this book, and by the time the transcriber reached the twelfth chapter he seems to have tired of his labours and to have made up his mind to conclude with a genealogical list of the Kiché kings. He here traces the genealogies of the three royal houses of Cavek, Nihaib, and Ahau-Kiché. The state of transition and turmoil in which the country was for many years after the conquest must have tended to the disappearance of native records of any kind, and our author does not appear to have been as well versed in the history of his country which immediately preceded his own time as he was in her mythology and legends. According to a tradition recited by Don Domingo Juarros in his "History of the Kingdom of Guatemala," the Toltecs emigrated from the neighbourhood of Tula in

Mexico by direction of an oracle, in consequence of the great increase of population in the reign of Nimaquiché, fifth King of the Toltecs. "In performing this journey they expended many years and suffered extraordinary hardships." Nimaquiché was succeeded by his son Aexopil, from whom was descended Kicab Tanub, the contemporary of Montezuma II. This does not at all agree with the "Popol Vuh" account.

COSMOGONY OF THE "POPOL VUH"

THE COSMOGONY OF the "Popol Vuh" exhibits many signs of Christian influence, but it would be quite erroneous to infer that such influence was of a direct nature; that is, that the native compiler deliberately infused into the original narrative those outstanding features of the Christian cosmogony, which were undoubtedly quite familiar to him. The resemblance which is apparent between the first few chapters of the "Popol Vuh" and the creation-myth in Genesis is no more the result of design than was the metamorphosis of King Arthur's Brythonic warriors into Norman knights by the jongleurs. The inclusion of obviously Christian elements was undoubtedly unconscious. A native Guatemalan, nurtured in the Christian faith, could, in fact, quite be expected to produce an incongruous blending of Christian and pagan cosmogony such as is here dealt with.

But another and more important question arises in connection with the initial chapters of the "Popol Vuh"—those which give an account of the Kiché creation-myth. Under the veneer of Biblical cosmogony the original myth would appear to be the sum of more than one native creation-story. We have here a number of beings, each of whom appear in some manner to exercise the function of a creator, and it might be gathered from this that the account now before us was produced by the fusion and reconciliation of more than one legend connected with the creation—a reconciliation of early rival faiths. We have to guide us in this the proved facts of a composite Peruvian cosmogony. The ruling Inca caste skilfully welded together no less than four early creation-myths, reserving for their own divine ancestors the headship of the heavens. And it is not unreasonable to believe that the diverse ethnological elements of which the Maya-Kiché people were undoubtedly composed possessed divergent cosmogonies, which were reconciled to one another in the later traditional versions of the "Popol Vuh."

This would lead to the further supposition that the "Popol Vuh" is a monument of very considerable antiquity. The fusion of religious beliefs is, even with savages, a work of many generations. It would be rash to attempt to discover any approximate date for the original conception of the "Popol Vuh." The only version which we possess is that now under review, and as the lack of an earlier version makes comparison impossible, we are thus without the guidance with which the criteria of philology would undoubtedly furnish us. That the Mayan civilisation was of very considerable antiquity is possible, although no adequate proof exists for the assumption. This much is certain: that at the period of the Conquest written language was still in a state of transition from the pictographic to the phonetic-ideographic stage, and that therefore no version of the "Popol Vuh" which had been fixed by its receiving literary form could have long existed. It is much more probable that it existed for many generations by being handed down from mouth to mouth—a manner of literary preservation exceedingly common with the American peoples. The memories of the natives of America were and still are matter for astonishment for all who come into contact with them. The Conquistadores were astounded at the ease with which the Mexicans could recite poems and orations of stupendous length, and numerous instances of Indian feats of mnemonics are on record.

It is worthy of notice that the Kiché myth embodies the general aboriginal idea of creation which prevailed in the New World. In many of them the central idea of creation is supplied by the brooding of a great bird over the dark primeval waste of waters. Thus the Athapascans thought that a mighty raven, with eyes of fire and wings whose clapping was as the thunder, descended to the ocean and raised the earth to its surface.[1] The Muscokis believed that a couple of pigeons, skimming the surface of the deep, espied a blade of grass upon its surface, which slowly evolved into the dry land.[2] The Zuñis imagined that Awonawilona, the All-father, so impregnated the waters that a scum appeared upon their surface which became the earth and sky.[3] The Iroquois said that their female ancestor, expelled from heaven by her angry spouse, landed upon the sea, from which mud at once arose. The Mixtecs imagined that two winds—those of the Nine Serpents and the Nine Caverns—under the guise of a bird and a winged serpent respectively, caused the waters to subside and the land to appear. The Costa Rican Guaymis related, according to Melendez, that Noncomala waded into the water and met the water-nymph Rutbe, who bore him twins, the sun and moon. In all these accounts, from widely divergent nations, it is surprising to note such unanimity of belief; and when the tenacity of legend is borne in mind, it is perhaps not too rash to state a belief in an original American creation myth, which seems none the less possible, when the fact of the ethnological unity among the American tribes is remembered.

---

[1] "History of the Fur Trade," Mackenzie, p. 83.
[2] Schoolcraft, "Indian Tribes," i. p. 266.
[3] Cushing, "Zuñi Creation Myths."

It is by no means difficult to satisfactorily prove the genuine American character of the "Popol Vuh." In its case reading is believing. Macpherson, in his preface to the first edition of the poems of Ossian, says of an "ingenious gentleman" that ere he had read the poems he thought and remarked that a man diffident of his abilities might well ascribe these compositions to a person living in a remote antiquity; but when he had perused them his sentiments were changed. He found they abounded too much with those ideas that only belong to an early state of society to be the work of a modern poet. However this may apply to the reputed compositions of the Goidelic bard, there can be no doubt that it can be used with justice as regards the "Popol Vuh." To anyone who has given it a careful examination it must be abundantly evident that it is a composition that has passed through several stages of development; that it is unquestionably of aboriginal origin; and that it has only been influenced by European thought in a secondary and unessential manner. The very fact that it was composed in the Kiché tongue is almost sufficient proof of its genuine American character. The scholarship of the nineteenth century was unequal to the adequate translation of the "Popol Vuh"; the twentieth century has as yet shown no signs of being able to accomplish the task. It is, therefore, not difficult to credit that if modern scholarship is unable to properly translate the work, that of the eighteenth century was unable to create it; no European of that epoch was sufficiently versed in Kiché theology and history to compose in faultless Kiché such a work as the "Popol Vuh," breathing as it does in every line an intimate and natural acquaintance with the antiquities of Guatemala.

The "Popol Vuh" is not the only mythi-historical work composed by an aboriginal American. In Mexico Ixtlilxochitl, and in Peru Garcilasso de la Vega, wrote exhaustive treatises upon the history and customs of their native countrymen shortly after the conquests of Mexico and Peru, and hieroglyphic records, such as the "Wallam Olum," are not unknown among the North American Indians. In fact, the intelligence which fails to regard the "Popol Vuh" as a genuine aboriginal production must be more skeptical than critical.

KICHÉ AND MEXICAN MYTHOLOGY

THE CONNECTION OF Kiché and Mayan mythology with that of Mexico is obvious, but not altogether proven. It is possible that the main lines of the three systems were similar; that certain great deities like Gucumatz were common to all, but that the inclusion of local gods lent a very different complexion to the three mythologies. It also seems not unreasonable to suppose that the Kiché people must have been more liable to influence from the south, that is, from the north of South America. The inclusion of an Antillean deity (Hurakan) in their pantheon practically proves that they were, and their relative proximity to the Caribs—the great maritime race of America—leads to the assumption that they may have been influenced by those roving merchants and sailors more or less profoundly. This, however, can only be matter for surmise, and, however strong the probabilities seem in favour of such a theory, proof is wanting to strengthen it.

THE PANTHEON OF THE "POPOL VUH"

IT MUST BE remembered that we are dealing with Kiché and not with Mayan mythology. Although the two had much in common, it would be most unsafe in the present state of knowledge to attempt to identify Kiché with Mayan deities; such an attempt would, indeed, assume the bulk of a formidable treatise. Scholarship at the present time hesitates to designate the representations of Mayan gods on the walls of "buried" cities otherwise than by a letter of the alphabet, and it is therefore wise to thoroughly ignore the question of Mayan affinities in dealing with myths purely Kiché. This does not apply to the Kiché-Mexican affinities. Mexican and Kiché deities are mostly known quantities, but this cannot be said of their Mayan congeners. The reason for this is that until Mayan myth is reconciled with the evidence of the Mayan monuments no certitude can be arrived at. This cannot well be achieved until the Mayan hieroglyphs give up their secret, a contingency of which there is no immediate likelihood. Bearing this in mind, we may proceed to a brief consideration of the Kiché pantheon and its probable Mexican affinities.

Almost at the beginning we encounter a pair of masculine-feminine beings of a type nearly hermaphroditic, named Xpiyacoc and Xmucane, who are credited with a considerable share of the creation of organic life in the Kiché cosmogony. These, we will remember, appeared in the myth of

Vukub-Cakix and elsewhere. The first appears to apply to the paternal function, whilst the name Xmucane is derived from words signifying "feminine vigour," The Mexican equivalents of these gods were probably Cipactonatl and Oxomoco, the "father and mother gods.'"*

Deities who early arrest our attention are Tepeu, Gucumatz and Hurakan. The name of the first signifies "king." According to Brinton this in Kiché applies to rulership chiefly, inasmuch as the conjugal prowess often ascribed to monarchs by savage people is concerned. A creative faculty is obviously indicated in the name, but Brinton assumes that this Kiché generic name for king can also be rendered "syphilitic," especially as the name of the Mexican sun-god Nanahuatl has a similar significance.

That Tepeu was a generative force, a creative deity, there can be no doubt, but strangely enough in certain passages of the "Popol Vuh" we find him praying to and rendering homage to Hurakan, the "Heart of Heaven." We also find the latter along with Xpiyacoc, Xmucane and Tepeu jointly and severally responsible for the creation of the mannikins, if not for the whole cosmological scheme. This, of course, bears out the assumption of a composite origin of the creation-myth in the "Popol Vuh," but it is nevertheless strange to find Hurakan, whom we must reckon an alien deity, at the head of these Olympic councils.

Gucumatz is one and the same with the Nahuatlacan—or, more properly speaking, Toltecan Quetzalcohuatl. The name is compounded from two Kiché words signifying "Feathered Serpent," and its meaning in the Nahuatl is precisely the same. Concerning the nature of this deity, there is probably more difference of opinion than in the case of any other

---

* See Note 4, p. 56.

known to comparative mythology. Strangely enough, although unquestionably an alien in the mythology of the Aztecan branch of the Nahuatlacâ, he hulks more largely in the myths of that people than in the legends of the Kichés. To the Aztecâ he seems to have appeared as a half-friendly Baal, to worship or revile according to the opportunism of national fortune. If he were here to be dealt with as his importance demands the limits of this monograph would speedily be surpassed. Although unquestionably the same god to both Mexicans and Kichés, he had acquired a significance in Aztecan eyes quite out of all proportion to his Kiché or Mayan importance. To the Aztecan mind he was a culture-hero, unalterably associated with the sun, and with the origins of their civilisation. To the Toltecs he was the "Man of the Sun," the traveller, who, with staff in hand, symbolised the daily journey of the Sun-god. In all likelihood Quetzalcohuatl was evolved upon Mexican soil by the Toltecs, perhaps adopted from some older cults by them. He was at least worshipped sedulously by aboriginal or pre-Aztecan tribes in Anahuac. Mr. Payne writes:[1] "The fact that the worship of Quetzalcohuatl under the name of Cuculcan or Gucumatz was extensively prevalent in Yucatan and Central America, while no trace is found of the worship of Tezcatlipoca, strongly suggests that the founders of the Central American pueblos (the Toltecs) were, in fact, devotees of Quetzalcohuatl, who preferred exile and adventure in strange lands to accepting a religious innovation which was intolerable to them."

That Quetzalcohuatl was not an aboriginal Maya-Kiché deity is proved by the relative importance granted him by a people—the Aztecâ—to whom he was alien; and that they

---

[1] History of the New World.

regarded him as the aboriginal god of Anahuac *par excellence* is indisputable.

Hurakan, the winged creative power, is the wind of the tempest.[1] In the "Popol Vuh" he is designated "The Heart of Heaven." He is parallel with if not identical to the Aztecan deity Tezcatlipoca, who in his variant of Yoalli-ehecatl (the Wind of Night) was supplicated by the Aztecâ as the life-breath.[2] Elsewhere we have hinted that Tezcatlipoca may have been an ice-god.[3] Mr. Payne sees in him an elaboration of the vision of death in a polished "scrying"-stone, which seems possible but scarcely probable. Hurakan was in all likelihood derived from an original deity of the Antilles.[4] The term "hurricane" is said to have originated from the name of this god, and although the direct evidence for this is scanty, other circumstances place the connection beyond reasonable doubt. Hurakan is also alluded to in the "Popol Vuh," as "The Strong Serpent," and "He who hurls below," referring to his presence in the lightning. Brinton is of the opinion that the name Hurakan signifies "giant," but the sequence of proof is not altogether convincing. Hurakan had the assistance of three demiurges, named respectively Cakulha-Hurakan (lightning), Chipi-Cakulha (lightning-flash), and Raxa-Cakulha (track-of-the-lightning).

Hun-Ahpu and Xbalanque, who appear in the first myth proper—that of the destruction of Vukub-Cakix, are certainly "of the gods," but seem to be only demigods. They are constantly alluded to as "young men." Brasseur de Bourbourg,

---

[1] Oviedo, "Historia del l'Indie," lib. vi. cap. iii.
[2] Sahagun, lib. ii. ch. ii.
[3] "Mythologies of Ancient Mexico and Peru ("Religions Ancient and Modern" series).
[4] Oviedo, Brasseur de Bourbourg.

who saw in the Vukub-Cakix myth the struggle between the
Toltecs and the invading Nahuatlacâ, believed these hero-
gods to be equivalents of Tezcatlipoca and Nanahuatl, but
the resemblance appears to exist merely in the martial
character of the deities, and is hardly noticeable in other
details. Hun-Ahpu would appear to signify "The Master,"
but Brinton translates the name as "Magician." It may have a
reconciliatory translation as "Adept." A variant is the name
of his father Hun-Hun-Ahpu, "Each-one-a-Magician," and
some confusion is apparent in the Vukub-Cakix myth
between the two names; but as the Abbé Brasseur de
Bourbourg so justly observes, "these names are so symbolic
in character that their absolute elucidation is impossible."
Xbalanque signifies "Little Tiger."

"The gods of the Kichés were legion," but the foregoing
list embraces practically all the deities proper with whom we
have to deal in the "Popol Vuh."

THE VUKUB-CAKIX MYTH

The outstanding point of interest in the myth of Vukub-
Cakix and his two sons is its terrestrial significance. That
they were of the earth as truly as were the Jotuns of
Scandinavian mythology there can be no doubt. Like the
Jotuns or the Titans, Vukub-Cakix and his progeny are
made from the earth, and the parent giant is a living
representation of its surface. Xpiyacoc and Xmucane remove
his emerald teeth, and replace them with maize grains—
surely a mythical interpretation or allegory of the removal of
the green virgin turf of the earth, and its replacement by the
maize seed. It is further worthy of notice that the maize is
placed in Vukub-Cakix's mouth by divine beings. In the
third book of the "Popol Vuh" it is stated that the gods gave

maize to man. It was, indeed, brought to earth from heaven by the sacred animals.

BOOK II. COMMENTED UPON

The Second Book of the "Popol Vuh" is the most interesting of the four from a mythological point of view. That it treats of the dealings of the Kichés with the aboriginal people of the district they afterwards inhabited is not unlikely. Although the opinion of Brasseur that Xibalba was a prehistoric state which had Palenque for its capital is an exaggeration of whatsoever kernel of fact may be contained in the myth, yet it is not unlikely that the Abbé, who so often astonishes without illuminating, has in this instance come near the truth. The cliff-dwellings of Mexico and Colorado have of late years aroused speculation as to the aboriginal or directly prehistoric peoples of these regions. The "Popol Vuh" definitely describes Xibalba as the metropolis of an "Underworld"; and with such examples as that of the Cliff Palace Canon in Colorado before us, it is difficult to think that allusion is not made to some such semi-underground abode. There the living rock has been excavated to a considerable distance, advantage being taken of a huge natural recess to secure greater depth than could possibly have been attained by human agency, and in this immense alcove the ruins of a veritable city may still be seen, almost as well preserved as in the days of its evacuation, its towers, battlements and houses being as well marked and as plainly discernible as are the ruins of Philæ. It is then not unreasonable to suppose that in a more northerly home the Kichés may have warred with a race which dwelt in some such subterranean locality. A people's idea of an "otherworld" is often coloured by the configuration of their own country.

One thing is certain: a hell, an abode of bad spirits as distinguished from beneficent gods, Xibalba was *not*. The American Indian was innocent of the idea of maleficent deities pitted in everlasting warfare against good and life-giving gods until contact with the whites coloured his mythology with their idea of the dual nature of supernatural beings.[1] The transcriber of the "Popol Vuh" makes this clear so far as Kiché belief went. Dimly conscious that the "Popol Vuh" was coloured by his agency with the opinions of a lately adopted Christianity, he says of the Lords of Xibalba, Hun-Came and Vukub-Came: "In the old times they did not have much power. They were but annoyers and opposers of men, and, in truth, *they were not regarded as gods*." If not regarded as gods, then, what were they?

"The devil," says Cogolludo of the Mayas, "is called by them Xibilba, which means he who disappears or vanishes." The derivation of Xibalba is from a root meaning "to fear," from which comes the name for a ghost or phantom. Xibalba was, then, the Place of Phantoms. But it was not the Place of Torment, the abode of a devil who presided over punishment. The idea of sin is weak in the savage mind; and the idea of punishment for sin in a future state is unknown in pre-Christian American mythology.

"Under the influence of Christian catechising," says Brinton, "the Quiché legends portray this really as a place of torment, and its rulers as malignant and powerful; but as I have before pointed out they do so protesting that such was not the ancient belief, and they let fall no word that shows that it was regarded as the destination of the morally bad. The original meaning of the name given by Cogolludo points unmistakably to the simple fact of disappearance from among

---

[1] See Brinton, "Myths of the New World," Chap. ii.

men, and corresponds in harmlessness to the true sense of those words of fear, Scheol, Hades, Hell, all signifying hidden from sight, and only endowed with more grim associations by the imaginations of later generations.

The idea of consigning elder peoples, who have been displaced in the land to an underworld, is not uncommon in mythology. The Xibalbans, or aborigines, were perhaps cave- or earth-dwellers like the Picts of Scottish folk-lore, gnomeish, and full of elvish tricks, as such folk usually are. Vanished people are, too, often classed with the dead, or as lords of the dead. It is well known, also, that legend speedily crystallises around the name of a dispossessed race, to whom is attributed every description of magic art. This is sometimes accounted for by the fact that the displaced people possessed a higher culture than their invaders, and sometimes, probably, by the dread which all barbarian peoples have of a religion in any way differing from their own. Thus the Norwegians credited the Finns—their predecessors in Norway—with tremendous magical powers, and similar instances of respectful timidity shown by invading races towards the original inhabitants of the country they had conquered could readily be multiplied. To be tricked the barbarian regards as a mortal indignity, as witness the wrath of Thor in Jotunheim, comparable with the sensitiveness of Hun-Ahpu and Xbalanque lest they should be outwitted by the Xibalbans.

THE HARRYING OF XIBALBA

The doings of Hun-Ahpu and Xbalanque, in Xibalba, may be regarded either as the Kiché account of the adventures of two veritable heroes in a new land, or as the visitation of divine beings to Hades for the express purpose of conquering death. But by the period of the formation of the myth it is probable

that Xibalba had become confounded with the Place of the
Dead, and was regarded as a fit theatre for the prodigies of
craft and valour of the young hero-gods. The Kiché Hades
had, in fact, evolved from the old northern home, exactly as
had the Mexican Mictlan, which, although a subterranean
locality, was also, and separately, a northern country. A
complete Place of the Dead had been established, and the
gods, to how their contempt of death, must descend thereto
and emerge triumphant. The idea of metempsychosis was
known to the American aboriginal mind. "We Indians shall
not for ever die; even the grains of corn we put under the
earth grow up and become living things," is the noble and
touching reply of a chief to the interrogation of a Moravian
Brother, regarding the native belief in immortality.[1] Man
must have the example of the gods, if he wishes to live in
peace and quiet assurance of immortality. And just as we
believe that our God descended into Hell and vanquished Sin
and Death, so did these simple people gain strength to face
Eternity from the thought that they had been preceded in the
dark journey by the Immortals.

It is evident that the divine brothers feared ridicule, and
profiting from the disasters of their father and uncle made sure
of knowing the names of the chief Xibalbans ere they set out.
In like manner they avoided making an obeisance to the
dummy figures to which their predecessors had bowed so
profoundly. The American savage, grave and reserved, cannot
abide ridicule. He shrinks from it in a manner which a less
self-regarding or a more self-assured people cannot
comprehend. The other tests—the "House of Tigers," and
the "House of Cold," and the various torments mentioned in
the Second Book are much what might be expected from a

---

[1] Loskiel, "Ges. der Miss. der evang. Brüder."

barbarian idea of death—no more horrible, perhaps, than the European idea of Hell in the Middle Ages, certainly not more fear-compelling than the picture of Dante.

The American peoples are at one in their belief in a Paradise, a Place of Joy, if not of Reward. Their Hades appears to have been reserved almost entirely for the unillustrious. Paradise in some American mythologies, notably in that of Mexico, and perhaps in that of Peru, is nothing more than a preserve of the great; the poor might not enter therein, no more than might the coward pass the gates of the Norse Valhalla. It was to Mictlan or Supay, then, that the popular mind turned. How did the American peoples regard this drear abode? To enter it one must cross a deep and swift river by means of a bridge formed of a slender tree, said the Hurons and Iroquois to the first missionaries. On this frail passage the soul must defend itself from the attacks of a savage dog.[1] The Chepewayan Athapascans told of a great water which the soul must cross in a stone canoe; the Chilians, of a western sea, where toll must be given to an evil hag, who plucked out an eye if payment were not forthcoming; the Algonquins, of a stream bridged by an enormous snake. The Aztecs called this river Chicunoapa, the Nine Rivers, where the departed must pay toll to a dog and a dragon. It will be recollected that the brothers in the "Popol Vuh," cross a river of blood. This almost certainly alludes to the ocean under the red beams of the setting sun, towards which all these voyages are made.

The hero-gods in the myth voluntarily succumb to the power of the Lords of Death, and after being burned their bones are ground in a mill and thrown into the waters. The belief was almost universal in America that the soul resided in

---

[1] "Rel. de la Nouv. France," 1636.

the bones. The bones were the basis of the man. Flesh would readily perish, but would return to clothe this more lasting foundation. So in many tribes the bones of the dead were carefully preserved. In all Central American countries the bones of distinguished persons were preserved in temples or council-houses in the small chests made of cane mentioned by the chroniclers of De Soto's expedition. This, too, may possibly have been the origin of mummification in Peru. In Egypt all the members and intestines must be preserved, in Peru only the bones. The state of comparative desiccation in which most Peruvian mummies are discovered proves that the preservation of the flesh or organs was not regarded as a necessity.

The game of ball figures very largely throughout the Third Book. The father and uncle of the young hero-gods were worsted in their favourite sport by the Xibalbans, but Hun-Ahpu and Xbalanque in their turn vanquish the Lords of the Underworld. This may have resembled the Mexican game of tlachtli, which was played in an enclosed court with a rubber ball between two opposite sides, each of two or three players. It was, in fact, not unlike hockey. This game of ball between the Powers of Light and the Powers of Darkness is somewhat reminiscent of that between Ormuzd and Ahriman in Persian myth. The game of tlachtli had a symbolic reference to stellar motions.[1]

BOOK III. COMMENTED UPON

We are here engaged with the problem which the origin of man presented to the Kiché mind, and we shall find that its solution bears a remarkable likeness to that of similar American

---

[1] J. W. Fewkes in *Jour. Amer. Folk-lore,* 1892, p. 33; F. H. Cushing in "Amer. Anthropologist," 1892, p. 308 *et seq.*

myths. We seldom hear of one first-created being. In the creation-myths of the New World four brothers are usually the progenitors of the human race. Man in these myths is nearly always earth-born. He and his fellows emerge from some cavern or subterranean place, fully grown and fully armed. Thus the Blackfoot Indians emerged from Ninastahu, a peak in the Rockies. In the centre of Nunne Chaba, the High Hill, was a cavern, the house of the Master of Breath, whence came the Choctaws. The Peruvians came from Pacari Tambu, the House of the Dawn, near Cuzco, and an ancient legend of the Aztecâ states that they came from Chicomoztoc, the Seven Caverns, to, the north of Mexico.

We find the first Mayan men speedily engaged in migration. Such must always be the life of the unsettled and unagricultural savage. He multiplies. Gods are given to each tribe. These he bears to a new country. In fact we have a complete migration myth in the Third Book of the "Popol Vuh," and there are not wanting signs to show that this migration took place from the cold north to the warm south. The principal item of proof in favour of such a theory is, of course, the statement that the sun was "not at first born," and that at a later stage of the journey, when his beams appeared upon the horizon, it was as a weaker and dimmer luminary that he seemed to the wanderers than in after years. The allusion to "shining sand," by the aid of which they crossed rivers, may mean that they forded them when covered with ice. The whole myth is so strikingly akin to the Aztecân migration-myth given in the Mexican MS. in the Boturini Collection (No. 14, see. viii.) that we cannot refrain from appending a short passage from the latter:

"This is the beginning of the record of the coming of the Mexicans from the place called Aztlan. It is by means of the water that they came this way, being four tribes, and in coming they rowed in boats. They built their huts on piles at the place called the Grotto of Quinevayan. It is there from which the eight tribes issued. The first tribe is that of the Huexotzincos, the second tribe the Chalcas, the third the Xochimilcas, the fourth the Cuitlavacas, the fifth the Mallinalcas, the sixth the Chicimecas, the seventh the Tepanecas, the eighth the Matlatzincas. It is there where they were founded in Colhuacan. They were the colonists of it since they landed there, coming from Aztlan. . . . It is there that they soon afterwards went away from, carrying before them the god[1] Vitzillopochtli, which they had adopted for their god. . . . They came out of four places, when they went forward travelling this way. . . . There the eight tribes opened up our road *by water*."

We find a similar myth in the Wallam Olum, or painted records of the Lenape Indians. "After the flood," says this record, "the Lenape with the manly turtle beings dwelt close together at the cave house and dwelling of Talli. . . . They saw that the snake land was bright and wealthy. Having all agreed, they went over the water of the frozen sea to possess the land. It was wonderful when they all went over the smooth deep water of the frozen sea at the gap of snake sea in the great ocean" (Note 5).

We thus see that the Third Book of the "Popol Vuh" is a migration saga of a type not uncommon in America. Asiatic tribes may have come down from the Chi-Pixab of the "Popol Vuh" to British Columbia, and thence by easy stages to Central America. And the Third Book of the "Popol Vuh" may be the distant echo of a mighty wave of colonisation, whose sound swept the entire surface of the New World.

---

[1] In the Mexican text the Spanish word "diablo" has been interpolated by the Mexican scribes, as no Mexican word for "devil" exists. The scribe was, of course, under priestly influence; hence the "diablo."

EARLY SPANISH AUTHORS AND
THE "POPOL VUH"

IT CANNOT BE said that the early Spanish authors upon the affairs of Yucatan either corroborate or discredit the contents of the "Popol Vuh" in any way. To begin with, Landa, Cogolludo, and Las Casas confine themselves more to Yucatan proper than to Guatemala, and their remarks upon native belief, in so far as they illustrate the "Popol Vuh" at all, are really references to Mayan myths. Palacios is meagre in his references to any native beliefs, and the works of all four are so coloured by the phantasies of mediaeval theology that, although interesting, they possess little real value. So far, in fact, as they throw light upon the "Popol Vuh" they might be safely ignored, and they are only given as works of reference in the bibliography for the sake of completeness. They are, however, most valuable for the study of Mayan mythology proper, and for complete understanding of the "Popol Vuh" and of Kiché mythology in general, knowledge of Mayan myth is necessary.

EVIDENCE OF METRICAL COMPOSITION

THERE IS NOT wanting evidence to show that, like most barbarous compositions which depended for their popularity upon the ease with which they could be memorised, the "Popol Vuh" was originally composed in metre. Passages here and there show a decided metrical tendency, as:

> "Ama x-u ch'ux ri Vuch
> Ve, x-cha ri mama.
> Ta chi xaquinic
> Quate ta chi gekumarchic
> Cahmul xaquin ri mama
> Ca xaquin-Vuch" ca cha vinak vacamic.

which is translated:

> "Is the dawn about to be?
> Yes, answered the old man.
> Then he spread apart his legs.
> Again the darkness appeared.
> Four times the old man spread his legs.
> Now the opossum spreads his legs
> Say the people.[1]

The first line almost scans in iambics (English style), and the fifth is perfect, except for the truncation in the fourth foot.

---

[1] This passage obviously applies to a descriptive dance emblematic of sunrise.

The others appear to us to consist of that alternation of sustained feet—musically represented by a semibreve—with pyrrhics, which is characteristic of nearly all savage dance-poetry. Father Coto, a missionary, observes that the natives were fond of telling long stories and of repeating chants, keeping time to them in those dances of which all the American aboriginal peoples appear to have been so fond—and still are, as Baron Nordenskjold has recently discovered in the Aymara country. These chants were called nugum tzib, or "garlands of words," and although the native compiler of the "Popol Vuh" appears to have been unable to recollect the precise rhythm of the whole, many passages attest its original odic character.

NOTE.—The pronunciation of *x* in Kiché equals *sh*. *Ch* is pronounced hard, as in the Scottish "loch," and *c* hard, like *k*.

BIBLIOGRAPHICAL APPENDIX

THE VARIOUS WORKS which contain notices of the "Popol Vuh" and the kindred questions of Mayan and Kiché mythology are so difficult of access to the majority of readers that it has been thought best to divide them into two classes: (1) those which can be more or less readily purchased, and which are, naturally, of more recent origin; and (2) those which are not easy to come by, and which, generally speaking, are the work of Spanish priests and colonists of the sixteenth, seventeenth, and eighteenth centuries.

I

The work on the subject which is most easily obtained, and indeed the only work which gives the original Kiché text, is that of the Abbé Brasseur de Bourbourg, "Vuh Popol: Le livre sacré de Quichés et les mythes de l'antiquité Américaine." The Kiché text was translated by the assistance of natives into French, and the translation is more or less inaccurate. The notes and introduction must be read by the student with the greatest caution. It was published at Paris in 1861.

Ximenes' translation into Spanish of the "Popol Vuh" and that of Gavarrete are about of equal value, rather inaccurate, and accompanied by scanty notes. The title of the first is "Las Historias del Origin de los Indios de

Guatemala, par el R. P. F. Francisco Ximenes (Vienna, 1856), and of the second, "El Popol Vuh," (San Salvador 1905). This exhausts the list of works written exclusively concerning the "Popol Vuh." The other works of Brasseur and those of Brinton contain more or less numerous allusions to it, but references to it in standard works of mythology are exceedingly rare. The only other works which have a bearing upon the subject are those upon Mayan and Kiché mythology or which, among other matter, historical or political, refer to it in any way. The most important of these are:

DR. OTTO STOLL—"Ethnographie der Republik Guatemala."

"Ethnologie der Indianer Stämme von Guatemala."

SCHERZER—"Die Indianer von Santa Catalina Istlavacan."

MÜLLER—"Geschichte der Amerikanischen Ur-religion" (1855).

E. FÖRSTEMANN—"Commentary on the Maya Manuscript," in the Royal Public Library of Dresden. Translation from the German by S. Wesselhoeft and A. M. Parker (Harvard University, 1906).

E. SELER—"Uber den Ursprung der Mittelamerikan Kulturen" (1902).

"Ein Wintersemester in Mexico und Yucatan" (1903).

"Codex Fejerváry-Mayer" (Berlin, 1901).

P. SCHELLHAS—"Representation of Deities of the Maya Manuscripts," translated by S. Wesselhoeft and A. M. Parker (Cambridge, Mass., 1904).

CYRUS THOMAS—"The Maya Year," Washington, 1894. "Notes on Maya and Mexican Manuscripts."

W. FEWKES—"The God 'D' in the Codex Cortesianus," (Washington, 1895).

All these works relate more or less entirely to *Mayan* mythology, and are chiefly valuable as illustrating the connection between the Kiché and Mayan mythologies. It must be understood that this is not a list of works relating to *Mayan* antiquities, but only a list of such works as refer at the same time to Mayan and Kiché mythology.

The brief essay of the late Professor Max Müller upon the "Popol Vuh" is of little or no value except as a statement in favour of its authenticity. It gives little or no information concerning the work, and is, indeed, chiefly concerned with the authenticity and nature of North American picture-drawings.

II

The principal works of the older Spanish authors, which in any way relate to the myths of Maya-Kiché peoples, are:

LAS CASAS—"Historia de los Indias" (1552).

COGOLLUDO—"Historia de Yucathan" (1688).

DIEGO DE LANDA—"Relacion de los Cosas de Yucatan" (translated into French, and edited by Brasseur).

XIMENES—"Escolias à los Historias del origèn de los Indios" *(Circa,* 1725).

PALACIOS—"l'Description de la Provincia de Guatemala" (in the collection of Ternaux-Compans).

JUARROS—"Historia de Guatimala."

NOTES

NOTE 1.

Much that is absurd has been written concerning the antiquity of the ruined cities of Central America, and some authors have not hesitated to place their foundation in an antiquity beside which the pre-dynastic buildings of Egypt would appear quite recent. But that they were abandoned not long before the Columbian era is now generally admitted. *See* Winsor's "Narrative and Critical History of America," chap. iii., and the works of Charnay, Maler, Maudslay, and Gordon, for modern opinion upon the subject; also the various monographs contained in the more recent volumes of the U.S. Bureau of Ethnology's annual report. That a very respectable antiquity belongs to several sites is, however, certain; and competent authorities have not hesitated to ascribe to some of the ruins an age of not less than two thousand years.

NOTE 2.

Payne has made it abundantly clear to our mind that the original seat of the Nahuatlacâ (which included both Toltecs and Aztecs) was in British Columbia (see his "History of America," vol. ii. p. 373 *et seq.*). He thinks they there occupied a position southerly to that of the Athapascan stock, and were probably the first northern people to come into contact with tribes possessed of the maize plant. The knowledge of this staple, he infers, spread rapidly among the northern peoples, and induced them to hasten their southern colonisation, but it does not appear to us probable that this would be an inducement to a savage flesh-eating people averse to a life of agricultural labour. The whole question of prehistoric American migration, and of the gradual civilisation by maize of the peoples who came within its zone, is most admirably discussed in vol. xix. of "The History of North America," by W. J. Magee and Cyrus Thomas (Philadelphia, George Barrie and Sons), published March 1908. The knowledge contained in this work is the outcome of a lifetime's labour in the U.S. Bureau of Ethnology, and its learned authors have undoubtedly produced a monumental treatise which it will take many a generation of research to supersede, if, indeed, that is possible.

NOTE 3.

The authorities for the settlement of the Toltecs in Yucatan are the Tezcucan chronicler Ixtlilxochitl, and Torquemada, who both allege that the immigrants went to Campeachy and the south.

NOTE 4.

There appear to be grounds for believing that the parent deities Xpiyacoc and Xmucane are but derivations from Gucumatz, and represent the male and female attributes of that god. In the "Popol Vuh" they are spoken of as being "covered with green feathers," the usual description of Gucumatz; but it is, of course, possible that they may have received some of his attributes in the general jumble of myths which, we have attempted to show, exists in the first book. Gucumatz, it will be remembered, is Quetzalcohuatl in another form, and the latter is often represented in the papyri as having a woman sitting opposite to him. She does not, however, appear to be at all analogous to Messrs. Förstemann and Schellhas's "Goddess I," whom I take to represent the Mayan equivalent of Xmucane, and who wears on her head the knotted serpent, a reptile characteristic of Quetzalcohuatl.

NOTE 5.

The Wallam Olum (painted records) of the Leni Lenape Indians have often been called into question as regards their authenticity, but the evidence of Lederer, Humboldt, Heckewelder, Tanner, Loskiel, Beatty, and Rafinesque, all of whom professed to have seen them, rather discounts such unbelief in their existence. They consisted of picture-writings, or hieroglyphs, each of which applied to a whole verse, or many words. The ideas were, in fact, amalgamated in a compound system, and bear exactly the same relation to written language as the American tongues did to spoken language; that is, they were of an agglutinative type, a linguistic form where several words are welded into one. There are several series, one of which records the doings of the tribes immediately subsequent to the Creation. Another series relates to their doings in America, and consists of seven songs, four of sixteen verses of four words each, and three of twenty verses of three words each. "It begins at the arrival in America," says Rafinesque ("The American Nations"), "and is continued without hardly any interruption till the arrival of the European colonists towards 1600." But this second series is a mere meagre catalogue of kings.